# MACBETH RECONSIDERED

BY

J. P. KEMBLE

**AMS PRESS**
NEW YORK

# MACBETH RECONSIDERED;

## A N

# E S S A Y:

### INTENDED

## AS AN ANSWER TO PART

### OF THE

## R E M A R K S

### ON SOME OF THE

## C H A R A C T E R S

### O F

## S H A K S P E A R E.

———————————

## L O N D O N:

PRINTED FOR T. AND J. EGERTON, WHITEHALL.

MDCCLXXXVI.

**Library of Congress Cataloging in Publication Data**

Kemble, John Philip, 1757-1823.
    Macbeth reconsidered.

    Published in a greatly revised form in 1817 under
title:  Macbeth and King Richard the Third.
    1.  Whately, Thomas, d. 1772.  Remarks on some of the
characters of Shakespeare.  2.  Shakespeare, William,
1564-1616--Characters.  I.  Title.
PR2989.W55  1972        822.3'3              70-144645
ISBN 0-404-03646-5

Reprinted from an original copy in the collections
of the George Peabody Department of the Enoch Pratt
Free Library

From the edition of 1786, London
First AMS edition published in 1972
Manufactured in the United States of America

AMS PRESS INC.
NEW YORK, N. Y.      10003

TO

EDMUND MALONE,

THIS

E   S   S   A   Y

IS

INSCRIBED

BY

HIS   OBEDIENT,

AND

OBLIGED   SERVANT,

THE AUTHOR.

## Advertisement to the Reader.

THE Passages printed in Italics are quotations from Mr. Wheatley's Remarks; and the references correspond with the edition of Shakspeare given by Johnson and Stevens 1778.

## MACBETH RECONSIDERED.

PLAYS are defigned, by the joint powers of precept and example, to have a good influence on the lives of men. Enquiries into the conduct of fable in the drama were ufelefs to this end: the regular, or irregular, difpofition of parts in a play is an artificial praife, or blame, that can contribute nothing to the improvement, or depravation, of the mind; for the caufe of morality is promoted only, when, by a cataftrophe refulting from principles natural to the agents, who produce it, we are taught to love virtue, and abhor vice.

Neglect of unity is the obvious fault of Shakfpeare's pieces, truth of manners their unrivalled excellence.

THIS

This Effay does not profefs to obferve upon any inconfiftency in the conduct of the tragedy of Macbeth, it concerns itfelf only with the fentiments of the hero of it, prefuming they will more effectually ferve ethicks, if, in analyfing his character, it fhews that there is no diftinction between him and king Richard, in the quality of perfonal courage., If Macbeth be what Mr. Wheatley defcribes him, we muft forego our virtuous fatisfaction in his repugnance to guilt, for it arifes from mere cowardice; and can gain no inftruction from his remorfe, for it is only the effect of imbecility; we defpife him; we cannot feel for him; and fhall never be amended by a wretch, who is uniformly the object of our contempt.

The writer of thefe pages does not confider, that his pofition will never be eftablifhed, till Mr. Wheatley's be overthrown, without perceiving how difficult, and apparently invidious, a tafk he undertakes; he relies, however, upon Shakfpeare to clear Macbeth from the imputation laid on his nature; and can truly fay, the argument is not taken up in a fpirit of controverfy, but out of a love for, what is believed to be, juft criticifm.

Having

Having given many judicious proofs of the difference, there certainly is, in the characters of Macbeth and Richard, Mr. Wheatley proceeds to the article of courage, and fays, *In Richard it is intrepidity, and in Macbeth no more than refolution: in him* [Macbeth] *it proceeds from exertion, not from nature; in enterprize he betrays a degree of fear, though he is able, when occafion requires, to ftifle and fubdue it.*

The attempt to controvert this doctrine naturally refolves itfelf into three heads; namely, a repetition of the fimple character of Macbeth, as it ftands before any change is effected in it by the fupernatural foliciting of the weird fifters; a confideration of his conduct towards Banquo, and Macduff; and a review of his deportment, as oppofed to Richard's in the " Remarks." This order will involve an inquiry into Mr. Wheatley's interpretation of the poet's text; into the appofitenefs of the facts adduced in fupport of his opinion; and into his philofophy of the peculiar paffion of characters, when, facts not fupplying teftimony, he can fubftantiate his hypothefis only on the evidence of appropriated fentiment.

An appeal for judgement on the nature of Macbeth's courage lies to the tribunal of

Shakfpeare

Shakfpeare himfelf. The circumfcribed nature of a drama renders it generally impracticable for the principal perfonages in it gradually to unfold themfelves ; it is, therefore, an allowed artifice with dramatic authors (and of which they commonly avail themfelves) by an impreffive defcription of their heroes to bring us, in a great meafure, acquainted with them, before they are actually engaged in fcenes, where, for want of fuch previous intelligence, their proceedings might appear, at beft, confufed, and generally, perhaps, inexplicable. We are bound, then, to receive the introductory portrait our author has drawn of Macbeth as a true refemblance ; for a creature of the poet's arbitrary creation may be affimilated only to thofe features, which he has thought fit to give him. Here is the picture.

" —— The mercilefs Macdonel
" ——————————————
" —— from the weftern ifles
" Of kernes and gallow-glaffes is fupply'd ;
"And fortune, on his damned quarrel fmiling,
" Shew'd like a rebel's whore : but all's too weak ;
" For brave Macbeth, (well he deferves that name)
" Difdaining fortune, with his brandifh'd fteel,
" Which fmoak'd with bloody execution,
" Like

" Like valour's minion, carved out his paffage,
" 'Till he fac'd the flave :
" And ne'er fhook hands, nor bade farewel to him,
" 'Till he unfeam'd him from the nave to the chops."

(P. 446. v. 4.)

Could Shakfpeare call a man brave, and infift upon his well deferving that appellation; could he grace a man with the title of valour's minion, and deem him, as he does in a fubfequent paffage, worthy to be matched even with the goddefs of war ;—could he do this, and not defign to imprefs a full idea of the dignity of his courage ? Macbeth's great heart pants to meet the mercilefs leader of the rebels ; his executing fword, all dyed in reeking gore, hews out a paffage to him ; he maintains the combat, 'till the death of his antagonift crowns his perfiftive valour with the victory he burned for.

It is faid, Macbeth has *refolution*, not *intrepidity*. What is the foldier's intrepidity, but difdaining fortune ?

It is objected, though with fome qualification, that Macbeth's courage *proceeds from exertion, not from nature* ; and that in *enterprize he betrays a deal of fear*. Let us turn to the portrait once more.

" Cap.

" Cap. No fooner juftice had, with valour arm'd,

 " Compell'd thefe fkipping kernes to truft their
  heels ;

 " But the Norweyan lord, furveying vantage,

 " With furbifh'd arms, and new fupplies of men,

 " Began a frefh affault.

" King. Difmay'd not this

 " Our captains, Macbeth and Banquo ?

" Cap. Yes ;

 " As fparrows, eagles ; or the hare, the lion.".…

      (P. 449. v. 4.)

The Thane of Roffe takes up the narrative ;——

" Norway himfelf, with terrible numbers,

" ————————————————

" ———————— began a difmal conflict ;

" 'Till that Bellona's bridegroom, lapt in proof,

" Confronted him with felf-comparifons,

" Point againft point rebellious, arm 'gainft arm,

" Curbing his lavifh fpirit : and to conclude,

" The victory fell on us."————P. 452. v. 4.

Is it to betray fear in enterprize, already
worn with the fatigues of a hard-fought field,
to rufh, at difadvantage, on frefh fupplies and
terrible numbers, unconcerned as eagles, when
they fwoop on fparrows, and lions, when
they ftrike a hare ? It cannot be the laboured
effect of exertion, it is the fpontaneous im-
pulfe of a dauntlefs nature, that again hurries
Bellona's bridegroom, through all the horrors
of a difmal conflict, to fingle out and hold the
royal invader point againft point, till his re-
         fiftlefs

fiftlefs arm has curbed his lavifh fpirit, and
raifed on his difcomfiture the trophies of a
fecond conqueft.

Macbeth now enters in the fcene, and a
deputation from the fovereign meets him, with
thefe gracious acknowledgements to his tri-
umphant valour.

" The king hath happily received, Macbeth,
" The news of thy fuccefs : and when he reads
" Thy perfonal venture in the rebel's fight,
" His wonder and his praifes do contend,
" Which fhould be thine, or his : filenc'd with that
" In viewing o'er the reft o' the felf-fame day,
" He finds thee in the ftout Norweyan ranks,
" Nothing afraid of what thyfelf didft make,
" Strange images of death. As thick as tale,
" Came poft with poft ; and every one did bear
" Thy praifes in his kingdom's great defence
" ————————————— —————
" ——— For an earneft of a greater honour,
" He bade me, from him, call thee 1 hane of Cawdor."
(P. 464. v. 4.)

The king congratulates Macbeth on his
fuccefs; and profeffes, that the praife, due
to his perfonal venture in the firft battle, is
loft in filent wonder at the fublimity of his
daring. How inexpreffible, then, are Duncan's feelings, when he finds him once more
engaged, the felf-fame day, in the ftout

C                    Norweyan

Norweyan ranks, carelefs of meeting that
death, which he was fo terribly dealing on
the fquadrons that furrounded him! The
king confers the forfeited honours of the
difloyal Cawdor upon his general, only as a
token of thofe higher dignities, which all
confpire to think his atchievements in the
kingdom's great defence have juftly merited.

Such is the character Shakfpeare attributes
to Macbeth, while yet the purenefs of his
confcience is uncontaminated by guilt. The
impetuofity of Glamis is the decifion of intrepidity ; the feats of his own hand affure to
him the renown of gallantry ; and the whole
tenour of his conduct, throughout this peril-
ous adventure, unequivocally difplays a foul,
that, with Othello's, may

" ———————— agnize
" A natural and prompt alacrity
" It finds in hardnefs."————(P. 465. v. 10.)

We come now to the fecond part of this
queftion. The " Remarks" affirm, that
*Macbeth is perfonally afraid of Banquo,* and that
*his fear is founded on the fuperior courage of the
other.*

The evidence, which is given in, of Banquo's fuperior courage may, perhaps, on ex-
amination,

amination, feem but of little weight. Whence
are the proofs of Macbeth's cowardice to be
brought? Not from his behaviour in battle.
It does not appear, that, *upon the firſt meeting of the witches, Macbeth is agitated much
more than Banquo*; Banquo's deſcription of
their figures, and his *ſeveral pertinent queſtions*
to them (amounting, though, to no more
than two) are not expreſſive of *mere curioſity*,
but of the ſurprife, with which himſelf and
his partner are equally affected, on their un-
expectedly encountering three objects of ſo
grotefque an appearance.

" ————————— What are theſe,
" So wither'd, and ſo wild in their attire;
" That look not like the inhabitants o' the earth,
" And yet are on't?—Live you? or are you ought
" That man may queſtion?————(P. 406. v. 4.)

If Macbeth *only repeats the ſame inquiry*, it is not
from timidity, but from a wifh for the fame
information; and when he does it *ſhortly*, he
indicates his impatience for an anſwer.

Why fhould the fpeeches of Macbeth and
Banquo, in this fcene, *appear to be injudiciouſly
diſtributed?* And how will *the difference in their
characters account for ſuch a diſtribution?* Banquo addreſſes the witches firſt: Banquo is

made

made to fee them firft; not in token of fuperiority, but merely, perhaps, that their
ceremonious filence to him,

" ———— each at once her choppy finger laying
" Upon her fkinny lips,"————(P. 406. v. 4.)

may heighten the folemnity of the pro-
phetic greeting, with which they' are about
to hail Macbeth. Yet, the diftribution of the
parts is of fo little moment, that it might
have happened fortuitoufly : to have done,
however, with conjecture, the context evinces,
that it is not produced for the purpofe of fhew-
ing Banquo's fuperiority, in *being perfectly calm
under an occurrence, that has ruffled* Macbeth.

If Macbeth *is amazed, when he fees the
witches are vanifhed,* and likens their difap-
pearance to the melting of breath into the
wind; Banquo is ftruck too, and compares
them, in their fudden evanefcence, to the
burfting bubbles of the water.—(P. 464. v.4.)

Banquo cannot be faid to *treat the witches
with contempt*; he adjures them,—

" I' the name of truth ;"————(P. 462. v. 4.)

and, with Macbeth, gives them, in fome fort,
credit for

" More than mortal knowledge."

" If

" If you can look into the feeds of time,
" And fay, which grain will grow, and which will
      not;
" Speak then to me, who neither beg, nor fear,
" Your favours, nor your hate."—(P. 462. v. 4.)

This is the language of manly firmnefs, not
of contempt. He does not mean to *ridicule*
*their prophecy* by anfwering to Macbeth's
queftion,

" Went it not fo?
" To the felf-fame tune, and words."—(P. 464. v. 4.)

This is a grave, and precife, reply to a particular, and interefting, demand. It has been
obferved, from the higheft critical authority,
that Malcolm confirms the ferious import of
the fpeech in queftion, when he calls the
effufions of Macduff's grief and rage a manly
" tune."—P. 586. v. 4.) It is plain, that
Banquo's exclamation——,

" What, can the devil fpeak true?"—(P. 465. v. 4.)

on hearing part of the prophecy fulfilled, is
dictated by wonder, not *difregard*; for, when
Macbeth takes occafion, from that very event,
to queftion him on the hope, he now might
                                    reafonably

reafonably entertain, of his family's advancement, he folemnly replies,

" ——————— 'Tis ftrange;
" And oftentimes, to win us to our harm,
" The inftruments of darknefs tell us truths;
" Win us with honeft trifles, to betray us
" In deepeft confequence."—(P. 466. v. 4.)

Now let us advert to the fubfequent effect,
which the declarations of the fifters have upon
Banquo's mind : he prays to be delivered from
their temptations;

" ——————— Merciful powers !
" Reftrain in me the curfed thoughts, that nature
" Gives way to in repofe !"—(P. 492. v. 4.)

Mr. Stevens, to whom every admirer of
Shakfpeare muft feel himfelf under high obli-
gations, obferves upon this paffage, " it is ap-
" parent from what Banquo fays afterwards"
—[to Macbeth, " I dreamt laft night of the
three weird fifters,"]— " that he had been
" folicited in a dream to attempt fomething,
" in confequence of the prophecy of the
" witches, that his waking fenfes were
" fhock'd at."—(P. 492. v. 4.) ——Thefe
horrible emotions could never have been
caufed

caufed in him by declarations, which he had
contemned, ridiculed, or difregarded. The
adventure on the heath, therefore, does not
prove Banquo's fpirit greater than Macbeth's.
The " Remarks" proceed thus, in proof
of Macbeth's perfonal fear of Banquo ; *his
principal object is the death of the father ; and the
fecuring of his crown againft Banquo's iffue, who
alone were pointed out to his jealoufy by the witches,
is no more than a fecondary confideration.*
Macbeth, when he *confeffes to Lady Macbeth, that his mind is full of fcorpions,* fhews
Banquo not to be the fole caufe of his un-
eafinefs, by adding, " Thou know'ft, that
Banquo, and his Fleance, lives :" Moreover ;
directing the affaffins, he tells them, the fon's
abfence is " no lefs material" to him, than
the father's ; he urges the death of Fleance
on a motive diftinct from cowardice; for,
allowing, one moment, that he perfonally
fear'd Banquo, it is impoffible to conceive he
could have felt the fame dread of a boy :
again ; had his fears been perfonal they muft
have ended with the removal of the object of
them ; but finding the fon has not fallen with
the father, he is again involv'd in all his
former apprehenfions.

" Fleance is 'fcap'd. )
" Then comes my fit again."—(P. 538. v. 4.)

The witches, it is true, only point out Banquo's iffue to Macbeth's jealoufy; but actual is not poffible progeny, and the lofs of one child does not prevent a man from begetting others: thus, the fecuring of his crown againft Banquo's iffue is fo far from being a *fecondary*, that it is the tyrant's only, inftigation to this double murder.

The original idea of Macbeth's perfonally fearing Banquo feems founded on thefe words;

"————— our fears in Banquo
" Stick deep ;"——

and,

"————— There is none, but he,
" Whofe being I do fear."—(P. 522. v. 4.)

It will be effentially neceffary, towards explaining the fenfe of thefe ftrong lines, to follow the train of reafoning through the context of the fpeech, from which they are taken.

"————— To be thus, is nothing ;
" But to be fafely thus :—Our fears in Banquo
" Stick deep ; and in his royalty of nature
" Reigns that, which would be fear'd : 'Tis much he
     dares ;

" And

" And, to that dauntlefs temper of his mind,
" He hath a wifdom, that doth guide his valour
" To act in fafety. There is none, but he,
" Whofe being I do fear : and, under him,
" My genius is rebuk'd; as, it is faid,
" Mark Anthony's was by Cæfar. He chid the fifters,
" When firft they put the name of king upon me,
" And bade them fpeak to him ; then, prophet-like,
" They hail'd him father to a line of kings :
" Upon my head they plac'd a fruitlefs crown,
" And put a barren fceptre in my gripe,
" Thence to be wrench'd with an unlineal hand,
" No fon of mine fucceeding. If it be fo,
" For Banquo's iffue have I fil'd my mind ;
" For them the gracious Duncan have I murder'd ;
" Put rancours in the veffel of my peace
" Only for them ; and mine eternal jewel
" Given to the common enemy of man,
" To make them kings, the feed of Banquo kings !
" Rather than fo, come, fate, into the lift,
" And champion me to the utterance !—(ibid.)

In this foliloquy the ufurper reflects, that,
after all he has done to obtain the crown, he
is in great danger of lofing it ; weighs the
caufes of that danger ; and refolves, by re-
moving them, to take effectual meafures for
the firmly eftablifhing of his fupremacy. In
other words ;——

I have poffefs'd myfelf of the fovereignty ;
but to what avail, when, in a moment, it

D                                            may

may be wrefted from me? Banquo's eye is
fix'd upon it; and there reigns in his very
nature a royalty, that feems to realize his ex-
pectations: he is not only a foldier of uncom-
mon bravery, but fo confummate a politician,
that, fhould he revolt againft my govern-
ment, he would infallibly carry his defigns
fuccefsfully into execution. He is the only
man alive, whofe attempts I dread: and he
holds as high an afcendant over my good genius, as, it is faid, Cæfar did over Mark An-
tony's. His hopes are not only ftrengthen'd by
his natural endowments, but embolden'd too
by the affurances of prophecy: hearing me
faluted king by the fifters, he bade them fpeak
to him; they obey'd; and hail'd him father
to a line of kings; they plac'd a crown upon
my head, and put a fceptre in my hand, not
to be tranfmitted to my own, but to be
wrench'd away by the unlineal inheritance of
his, children. If fo, I fhall have perpetrated
fuch crimes, as muft embitter every moment
of my life in this world, and forbid every
hope of happinefs in the world to come, only
to make the feed of Banquo kings! It muft
not be—I here oppofe myfelf to the predic-
tion, and refolve by extirpating his family,
to elude the decrees of fate itfelf.

The

The ufurper, then, does not plunge into
freſh crimes *to get rid of perſonal fear*—ambition impels him to the murder of Duncan;
and the fame ambition urges him on the deſtruction of Banquo and Fleance, who feem
deſtin'd to degrade him and his houſe from
the ſplendors of monarchy to the obſcurity
of vaſſalage.

The " Remarks" find additional proofs of
Macbeth's cowardice in his conduct towards
Macduff—" *The fame motives of perſonal fear,
and thoſe unmix'd with any other, impel him to
feek the deſtruction of Macduff.*"

Macbeth is not wrought by *perſonal fear*, to
deſtroy Macduff, but by the knowledge of
his diſaffection,

" How fay'ſt thou, that Macduff denies his perfon,
" At our great bidding ?"—(P. 546. v. 4.)

The diſcontented Thane of Fife is a man,
whoſe parts and popularity are not to be de-
ſpis'd; he is deſcribed,

" ——— Noble, wife, judicious,"—(P. 567. v. 4.)

And Roſſe, ſpeaking of the misfortune that
had befallen him in the loſs of his wife and
children, fays,

D 2                                        " No

[ 20 ]

" No mind, that's honeft,
" But in it fhares fome woe."—(P. 584. v. 4.)

If Macbeth thanks the apparition, that had
" harped his fears aright,"—it is becaufe, its
caution juftifying his fufpicions, he fhall now
provide more ftrenuoufly againft the machina-
tions of his enemy.

If, when told that,

" ——— none of women born
" Shall harm him,—

he fays,

" Then live, Macduff;"—

yet, repreffing the feelings of confidence, inftantly adds,

" ——— Thou fhalt not live ;
" That I may tell pale-hearted fear it lies ;"—

the quality of that fear is decided, when
(being affur'd, that he

" ——— fhall never vanquifh'd be, until
" Great Birnam wood to high Dunfinane hill
" Shall come againft him,—)

he exclaims,

" ——— Our *high-plac'd* Macbeth
" Shall live the leafe of nature,"—(P. 562. v. 4.)

When

When the Thane of Fife encounters Macbeth in battle, the tyrant does not ufe the
power upon his life, which he believes himfelf poffefs'd of, as inftantly he would, had
he fear'd him; but, yielding to compunc-
tion for the inhuman wrongs he had done
him, wifhes to avoid the neceffity of add ng
Macduff's blood to that, already fpilt in the
flaughter of his deareft connections.

" ——— Get th e back, my foul is too much charg'd
" With blood of thine already.
" *Macd.* I have no words,
" My voice is in my fword ; thou bloodier villain
" Than terms can give thee out !—(*Fight.*)
" *Macb.* Thou lofeft labour :
" As eafy may'ft thou the intrenchant air
" With thy keen fword imprefs, as make me bleed :
" Let fall thy blade on vulnerable crefts;
" I bear a charmed life, which muft not yield
" To one of woman born."—(P. 606. v. 4.)

Unmov'd by Macduff's taunts and furious
attack, Macbeth advifes him to employ his
valour where fuccefs may follow it, and gene-
roufly warns him againft perfifting to urge an
unequal combat with one, whom deftiny had
pronounced invincible.—

The " Remarks" would now condemn
Macbeth from his own confeffion of the truth

of

of the accufations brought againft him——
" *That apprehenfion was his reafon for thefe*
" *murthers, he intimates himfelf; when meditating*
" *on that of Banquo, he obferves, that,*"

    " Things bad begun make ftrong themfeives by ill."—
                    (P. 535. a. 3. f. 2.)

" *And when that of Macduff is in contemplation,*
" *he fays,*"

    " ——————— I am in blood
    " Stept in fo far, that, fhou'd I wade no more,
    " Returning were as tedious as go o'er."—
                    (P. 546. v. 4.)

The comment on thefe paffages, which Cibber puts into the mouth of king Richard, is remarkable, and juftly explains their meaning.

    " Crowns got with blood muft be with blood main-
         tain'd." (Act 3.)

and,

    " When I look back, 'tis terrible retreating;
    " I cannot bear the thought, nor dare repent."-(Act 5.)

In a word, Macbeth does not meditate the deaths of Banquo and Macduff through " *per-*
" *fonal fear*" of them; but becaufe his ambition renders the former obnoxious to his envy, and the latter to his hatred.

                                  It

It muſt now be ſhewn, that the proofs of Richard's ſuperior courage are not concluſive againſt Macbeth. Equal firmneſs in equal trials will invalidate ſome of them; ſome are to be refuted by ſhewing that what is objected to Macbeth as timidity will as ſtrongly affect Richard himſelf; and ſome may, perhaps, be founded on miſapprehenſion of fact, or ſentiment.

If it is a mark of reſolution in Richard that, when Tyrrel informs him the princes are diſpatched, " *though certain of the event, he is* " *ſolicitous to hear at leiſure in what manner it* " *was conducted—*

    " Come to me, Tyrrel, ſoon at after ſupper,
    " When thou ſhalt tell the proceſs of their death ;"—
                 (P. 115. v. 7.)

Macbeth muſt be allowed to diſplay preciſely the ſame quality, when he ſays to the murderer, who has related to him the proceſs of Banquo's death,

    " ———— Get thee gone ; to-morrow
    " We'll hear, ourſelves again." (P. 558. v. 4.)

The " Remarks" proceed—" *Macbeth's* " *ſuſpicions extend to all his great lords—*

    " There is not a one of them, but in his houſe
    " I keep a ſervant fee'd ;"—(P. 546. v. 4.)
                     and,

and, " *he tells the phyſician,*"—

" The Thanes fly from me."—(P. 596. v. 4.)

Does not Richard betray as much ſuſpicion when he dares not truſt Stanley, till he has taken the young lord Strange as a ſurety for his fidelity ?—and is he not as anxious from a mere doubt of his followers, as Macbeth is on finding himſelf really deſerted?

> " *K. Rich.* O Ratcliff, I have dream'd a fearful
> dream !—
> " What think'ſt thou ?—Will our friends prove all
> true ?—
> " *Rat.* No doubt, my Lord.
> " *K. Rich.* I fear, I fear.
> " ——————————————————————
> " ——————————————————————
> " —————————— Come, go with me
> " Under our tents; I'll play the eaves-dropper,
> " To hear, if any mean to ſhrink from me."
>
> (P. 156. v. 7.)

Mr. W. ſays, " *His going round the camp, juſt before the battle, to liſten if any meant to ſhrink from him, is proper on that particular oc- caſion*"——Agreed—But why think the ſame action proper conduct in Richard, and cow- ardice in Macbeth ?—

The

The " Remarks," bent upon exalting
Richard at Macbeth's expence, fay, " *The*
" *fame determined fpirit carries him through the*
" *bloody bufinefs of murdering his nephews: and*
" *when Buckingham fhews a reluctance to be*
" *concern'd in it, he immediately looks out for*
" *another—Had Macbeth been thus difappointed*
" *in the perfon to whom he had open'd himfelf,*
" *it would have difconcerted any defign he had*
" *form'd.*"

It appears, however, that the perfons
Macbeth open'd himfelf to, were not wrought
to his purpofe on their firft interview; yet it
does not difconcert his defigns; he fends for
them again, repeats his former converfation,
and prevails with them by ftrong arguments,
and large promifes, to undertake a murder,
the execution whereof he fteadily perfifts in.
P. 325. v. 4.

Again, " *All the crimes Richard commits are*
*for his advancement, not for his fecurity.*

Richard removes Clarence and Haftings, as
Macbeth does Duncan, for his advancement;
but he murders his nephews and his wife, as
Macbeth does Banquo, to fecure himfelf in
that advancement.

E                         Why

Why fhould it be fuppofed Macbeth
" *catches the terrors he fees exprefs'd in the coun-*
" *tenance of the meffenger, who informs him of*
" *numbers of the enemy?*"

" *Ser.* There is ten thoufand ———
" *Macb.* Geefe, villain ?
" *Ser.* Soldiers, Sir.
" *Macb.* Go, prick thy face, and over-red thy fear,
" Thou lily-liver'd boy. What foldiers, Patch ?
" Death of thy foul ! thofe linen cheeks of thine
" Are counfellors to fear."—(P. 593. v. 4.)——

From the contemptuous manner in which
he treats the intelligence, he feems rather to
imagine what effect fuch looks might have
upon the garrifon, than to acknowledge any
they have produc'd upon himfelf—What is
Richard's compofure in a fimilar fituation ?
The information he receives of infurrections
in Devonfhire and Kent being followed by
news of Buckingham's army, ftriking the
meffenger, he exclaims,

" Out on ye owls !—nothing but fongs of death ?
" There, take thou that."—(P. 137. v. 7.)

Macbeth's courage is impeach'd, becaufe
" *he calls for his armour, notwithftanding Sey-*
" *ton's remonftrance, that*

" It is not needed yet"—

" *perfifts*

" *perſiſts in putting it on*; *calls for it again*
" *eagerly afterwards*; *bids the perſon who is*
" *aſſiſting him*

" Diſpatch"—

" *then, the moment it is on, pulls it off again,*
" *and directs his attendants to,*

" Bring it after."—(P. 597. v. 4.)

Is there more confuſion and inconfiſtency in this, than in the following, ſcene?

" *Rat.* Moſt mighty ſovereign, on the weſtern coaſt
" Rideth a puiſſant navy; to the ſhore
" Throng many doubtful hollow-hearted friends,
" Unarm'd and unreſolv'd, to beat them back:
" 'Tis thought, that Richmond is their admiral;
" And there they hull, expecting but the aid
" Of Buckingham to welcome them aſhore.
" *K. Rich.* Some light-foot friend poſt to the duke of Norfolk;—
" Ratcliff, thyſelf,—or Cateſby;—where is he?
" *Cates.* Here, my good lord.
" *K. Rich.* Cateſby, fly to the duke—
" *Cates* I will, my lord, with all convenient haſte.
" *K. Rich.* Ratcliffe, come hither: poſt to Saliſbury;
" When thou comeſt thither—Dull, unmindful villain,
                                    (To Cateſby.)
" Why ſtay'ſt thou here, and go'ſt not to the duke?
" *Cates.*

" *Cates.* Firſt, mighty liege, tell me your highneſs'
pleaſure,

" What from your grace I ſhall deliver to him.

" *K. Rich.* O, true, good Cateſby;—Bid him levy
ſtraight

" The greateſt ſtrength and power he can make,

" And meet me ſuddenly at Saliſbury.

" *Cates.* I go.

" *Rat.* What, may it pleaſe you, ſhall I do at Saliſbury ?

" *K. Rich.* Why, what would'ſt thou do there before I go ?

" *Rat.* Your highneſs told me, I ſhou'd poſt before,

" *K. Rich.* My mind is chang'd.—(P. 134, v. 7.)

Arguing principally from the recited in-
ſtances of it, the " Remarks" ſay, " *Theſe*
" *are all ſymptoms of timidity, which he confeſſes*
" *to have been natural to him, when he owns that*"

" The time has been my ſenſes wou'd have cool'd

" To hear a night-ſhriek, and my fell of hair

" Wou'd at a diſmal treatiſe rouſe and ſtir,

" As life were in't.—I have ſupt full of horrors ;

" Direneſs, familiar to my ſlaught'rous thoughts,

" Cannot once ſtart me."—(P. 599. v. 4.)

Here Mr. W. refutes his own poſition ;
for, if his interpretation of theſe lines be ad-
mitted, he muſt allow that Macbeth, what-
ever his former feelings were, has no timidity
in

in his difpofition now. But the paffage refers neither to fear or courage—it is a pathetic reflection on the dreadful change produced in his humane habits, during a feventeen years ufurpation, the records whereof are crouded with practices fo oppreffive and bloody, as have hardened his once eafily yielding temper againft all impreffions of fenfibility, and the charities of nature.

P. 76. When Richard " *afks*"

" My lord of Surry, why look you fo fad ?"—
(P. 144. v. 7.)

and afterwards " *enquires,*"

" Saw'ft thou the melancholy lord Northumberland?"
(P. 147. v. 7.)

he is not " *fatisfied upon being told, that he and*
" *Surry were bufied in*

" Chearing up the foldiers."—

He would, indeed, fain perfuade himfelf to be fatisfied ; but, in reality, he is far from being at eafe.

" I am fatisfied—Give me a bowl of wine :
" I have not the alacrity of fpirit,
" Nor cheer of mind, that I was won't to have."—
(P. 148. v. 7.)

The

The nature of Richard's queſtion on Surry's ſadneſs, and obſervation of Northumberland's melancholy, may be exemplify'd from Mr. W's judicious reflection on Macbeth's interrogatories to the phyſician———

" Canſt thou not miniſter to a mind diſeas'd ;
" Pluck from the memory, &c. &c.—"(P. 596. v. 4.)

" *Though it is the diſorder of Lady Macbeth that*
" *gives occaſion to theſe queſtions, yet,*————
" *in his own mind, he is all the while making*
" *application to himſelf.*
" *Richard repreſents the enemy as a troop of*
" *banditti* ;

" A ſort of vagabonds, raſcals, and run-aways,
" A ſcum of Brittains, and baſe lackey peaſants, &c."
(P. 165. v. 7.)

This harangue to his army ſhou'd not have been quoted as an inſtance of Richard's intrepidity ; for it does not contain his real ſentiments of Richmond's friends : the inferiority of the foe is a topic which generals, to encourage their own troops, have commonly affected ; and Richard never cou'd have ſeriouſly held in contempt ſuch enemies as

" Sir Walter Herbert, a renowned ſoldier ;
" Sir Gilbert Talbot, and Sir William Stanley ;
" Oxford,

" Oxford, redoubted Pembroke, Sir James Blunt,
" And Rice ap Thomas, with a valiant crew ;
" And many others of great name and worth.—
(P. 139. v. 7.)

When lady Macbeth, finding her hufband
will proceed no further in the bloody bufinefs
of his fovereign's death, reproaches him thus;

" ——————— Would'ft thou have that,
" Which thou efteem'ft the ornament of life,
" And live a coward in thine own efteem ;
" Letting I dare not wait upon I would——?"—
(P. 488. v. 4.)

his reply,

" I dare do all that may become a man"———

is fo far being an affertion of mere " *manlinefs*
" *of charaÉter*," in Mr. W's fenfe, that it
fublimely expreffes an entire contempt of
danger, and reverence for virtue.

To compare Macbeth and Richard under
the influence of vifions—Macbeth addreffes
Banquo thus,

" Why, what care I ? If thou can'ft nod, fpeak too.
" If charnel-houfes, and our graves, muft fend
" Thofe that we bury, back ; our monuments
" Shall be the maws of kites."—(P. 541. v. 6.)

Again,

Again,

> " What man dare, I dare:
> " Approach thou like the rugged Ruffian bear,
> " The arm'd rhinoceros, or the Hyrcan tyger,
> " Take any fhape but that, and my firm nerves
> " Shall never tremble : Or, be alive again,
> " And dare me to the defert with thy fword;
> " If trembling I inhabit, then proteft me
> " The baby of a girl. Hence, horrible fhadow !
> " Unreal mockery, hence !—(P. 543. v. 4.)

Notwithftanding the firmnefs of this defiance, it cannot be fuppos'd but Macbeth is as much terrify'd while he utters it, as Richard is, when, ftarting out of a dream in which the fouls of thofe he had murder'd had appear'd to him, he cries,

> " Have mercy, Jefu !—foft; I did but dream.—
> " O coward confcience, how doft thou afflict me !
> " The lights burn blue.—Is it not dead midnight ?
> " Cold fearful drops ftand on my trembling flefh, &c."
> (P. 154. v. 7.)

Superftition may be a fign of timidity— Macbeth's fuperftition is founded on the ftrong affurances of preternatural agents, whofe firft promifes to him had been made good—Richard condefcends to be affected by omens,

> " Richmond !—when I was laft at Exeter,
> " The mayor in courtfy fhew'd me the caftle,

" And

" And call'd it Rouge-mont: at which name I ftarted;
" Becaufe a bard of Ireland told me once,
" I fhou'd not live long after I faw Richmond."—
(P. 112. v. 7.)

Again ;

" The fun will not be feen to-day;
" The fky doth frown and lour upon our army.
" I wou'd thefe dewy tears were from the ground !"—
(P. 159. v. 7.)

It will be faid, and it will be granted, that
Richard prefently ftifles thefe emotions : it is
only afferted that he feels them, like Macbeth; and that Macbeth, like him, can over-
come them.—The wood of Birnam moves towards Dunfinane—The tyrant

" Doubts the equivocation of the fiend."— .

and, believing the laws of nature invented to
his ruin,

" Pulls in refolution."—

Inftantly, however, he fhakes off this mo-
mentary difmay,

" ——————— Blow, wind! come, wrack !
" At leaft we'll die with our harnefs on our back."—
(P. 604. v. 4.)

He rufhes upon the enemy—encounters Macduff—The fifters have palter'd with him;
he has done with belief in the juggling
fiends, and can rely upon himfelf—

F

" Though

" Though Birnam wood be come to Dunfinane,
" And thou oppos'd, being of no woman born,
" Yet I will try thy laft : before my body
" I throw my warlike fhield : lay on, Macduff;
" And damn'd be him that firft cries, hold, enough."
(P. 608. v. 4.)

This conduct in Macbeth is ftigmatized with the name of *defpair*.—It certainly is of the fame nature with Richard's determination ;

" ———— I have fet my life upon a caft,
" And I will ftand the hazard of the die."—
(P. 164. v. 7.)

The refolution of both tyrants in the battles, that decided their fate, is that mix'd effufion of grief, fhame, and pride, which cannot be denominated lefs than the defpair of innate bravery.

If Macbeth's behaviour is to be called cow-ardly, when, overpowered by the completion of the prophecies, he, for a moment, declines the combat with Macduff; fo muft Richard's, when he flies with Haftings before Warwick and Somerfet, leaving Edward to the mercy of the Lancaftrians.—P. 522. v. 6.

From the review of the characters of the ufurpers, it appears not to be true of Richard, that " *upon no occafion, however tremendous,* " *and at no moment of his life, however un-* " *guarded,*

" *guarded, does he betray the leaſt ſymptom of*
" *fear ;*"—or of Macbeth, that he " *is always*
" *ſhaken upon great, and frequently upon trivial*
" *occaſions.*"

Macbeth and Richard are each of them as
intrepid as man can be : yet, it may be ſaid
of each, without any derogation from that
character, that he is, at times, agitated with
apprehenſions. The Earl of Peterborough has
left it upon record, that intrepidity and ſenſe
of danger are by no means incompatible.

Having endeavour'd to prove, that Macbeth
has a juſt right to the reputation of intrepidity ; that he feels no perſonal dread of Banquo and Macduff; and that he meets equal,
not to ſay ſuperior, trials, as boldly as Richard ; it may be expected this eſſay ſhould attempt to ſhew in what the eſſential difference
between theſe great bad men conſiſts.

Ambition is the impulſe that governs every
action of Richard's life ; he attains the crown
by diſſimulation, that owns no reſpect for
virtue ; and by cruelty, which entails no re-
morſe on the valour, that wou'd maintain his
ill-acquir'd dignity. Ambition is the predo-
minant vice of Macbeth's nature ; but he gra-
tifies it by hypocriſy, that reveres virtue too
highly to be perfectly itſelf; and by murders,
the

the recollection whereof, at times, renders his valour, ufelefs by depriving him of all fenfe, but that of his enormous wickednefs. Richard's character is fimple, Macbeth's mix'd. Richard is only intrepid, Macbeth intrepid, and feeling. Richard's mind not being diverted by reflection from the exigencies of his fituation, he is always at full leifure to difplay his valour; Macbeth, diftracted by remorfe, lofes all apprehenfion of danger in the contemplation of his guilt; and never recurs to his valour for fupport, till the enemy's approach rouzes his whole foul, and confcience is repell'd by the neceffity for exertion.

The writer of the above pages cannot conclude without faying, he read the " Remarks " on fome of Shakfpeare's Characters" with fo much general pleafure and conviction, that he wifhes his approbation were confiderable enough to increafe the celebrity which Mr. Wheatley's memory has acquir'd from a work, fo ufefully intended, and fo elegantly perform'd.

## F  I  N  I  S.